Epicenter

Epicenter

Poems by Wendy Wisner

CustomWords

© 2004 by Wendy Wisner

Published by CustomWords
P.O. Box 541106
Cincinnati, OH 45254-1106

Typeset in Aldine 401 by WordTech Communications LLC, Cincinnati, OH

ISBN: 1932339159
LCCN: 2003109453

Poetry Editor: Kevin Walzer
Business Editor: Lori Jareo

Visit us on the web at www.custom-words.com

Author photo: Ania Mianowska
Cover photo: I.J. Witkind, USGS

ACKNOWLEDGMENTS

I wish to thank the following publications in which these poems, or versions of them, first appeared:

5 AM:	"December: Martha's Vineyard…"
Big City Lit:	"On Your Parents' Stoop"
	"We Went to the Moon"
Main Street Rag:	"Fourteen in His Attic"
Red River Review:	"Mariposa Avenue"
	"Record Player"
RUNES, A Review of Poetry:	"Nightgown"
Sojourner:	"Martha's Vineyard, 1980"

For their faith and guidance throughout the shaping of this book, I am deeply grateful to Donna Masini, Jan Heller Levi, Ashley Crout, Elizabeth Wilson, Amy Meckler, Dahlia Wisner, and Danny Pitt Stoller.

for my family

CONTENTS

I.

Martha's Vineyard, 1980 / 13
Calculator / 16
December / 18
Record Player / 19
Chest / 20
Boston Night I / 21
Camera / 23
December / 25
Boston Night II / 26

II.

Fresh Cut / 31
Jar of Seashells / 33
Redwood City / 34
The Inside of Houses / 35
Nightgown / 37
California Man / 38
Mariposa Avenue / 40
Oakland, '89: After the Earthquake / 42

Pennies / 45
First Blood / 46
East / 48

III.
Bride / 51
Fourteen in His Attic / 53
Endymion / 54
Marriage Vow / 56
Equinox / 58
Fall / 60
Thinking of My Father / 61
Lullaby / 62
A Husband's Things / 63
On Your Parents' Stoop / 65

IV.
Four Dreams / 69
We Went to the Moon / 71
Field /72

I.

MARTHA'S VINEYARD, 1980

It was the fall before John Lennon was killed.

Each night my father
sat in the hazy gray kitchen, lost
in the checkered tablecloth, the record

spinning, John's voice
weaving through the waves
of the ocean. He could float—

the monster—he would
stay with us, hovered
near the smoke alarm, curled

like a baby under the stove.
He was red. Like the red
cliffs, sand, red seagull

eye, moon, reefs, rocking.
My father said he was born
in our house, and would die there.

What did my mother think
of him, sleeping in our attic
on his great red stomach? I saw her

down the curved dirt path
behind a counter
frowning as she held out

chunk after chunk of bread.
How well she knew how hard it was
to wait, the bread growing

stale in her fingers, her apron
spotted with oil, one thread
loose, stuck like a tick to her thigh.

Did she sleep on the ocean bed, still
in her apron? I don't remember my parents
touching. Did she see the monster?

Did he love her? I never remembered
falling asleep in my father's arms. I never saw him
carefully holding my body

together, rocking me against his soft blue shirt, the moan
of John singing *I wanted you so bad*, the waves parting
as my mother got closer.

CALCULATOR

Abandoned in a dusty wicker basket,
on the kitchen table with my mother's things:
nail file, melon baller, vitamins, scissors, tweezers.
I believed my father used it
privately, in the middle of the night, his fingers
on the hard black buttons.
Waiting for dinner, or for nothing,
I'd grab it, I'd use it.
I loved the slim gray screen
lit in deep red numbers, I loved
the numbers, adding more,
more, I'd fill that screen, add each full screen
to another, add and add,
there were that many numbers,
there was room for my numbers
in whatever it was—a brain, a heart?—
under the plastic, the dust,
ticking—soon
the buttons were damp, cold wind
thrust through the window.

It was stuck, it was over.

The small *E* pulsed

and I put it back where I'd found it:

against my mother's vitamins, for my father.

DECEMBER

Martha's Vineyard. Paradise. The dark
living room. Sand and salt

in my mouth. Wanting water. Wanting
to ask for some. The words

he's dead it's John he's dead—
Someone screamed them.

Then footsteps. My mother
holding a glass of water. Her fingers

slipping, falling, pieces of glass
and water everywhere.

Praying. My father. His back to me.
Leaning over the record player.

John singing.

RECORD PLAYER

He dipped an orange rag in a glass of water
and slid it over the glass top.
Sometimes he would lift the top,
put his hand inside and tap the dust
off the needle, and if the power
was on (I think it always was) a thumping
filled the room, tender and electric,
my father's sound.

CHEST

I loved and feared
the dark wood, pennies
flickering in a bowl at the top.
I rocked my dolls to sleep
in the drawer I could reach
among black socks and undershirts
which smelled like his hair
when I sat on his shoulders,
gripped his neck with my thighs,
saw the world tilt
with my power.

BOSTON NIGHT I

We were brute that night.
If he left, we would remember it.
That's the way he loved us—
relentlessly, purposefully.

Sometimes I think of it
as a privilege, a terrible secret,
what we hid from the baby:

cold air dark around us,
the cave our kitchen had become,
my parents and I huddled
over the orange light
of the family garbage…

It needed emptying.
I remember thinking *this is it*.
I looked at their faces.
I knew they loved each other.

You know these things
the night your father leaves—

the way we felt the first time
we made fire: *it is ours, it is good.*

Tell me what my father felt
    vanishing
into the white Boston night,
the arms of California.

CAMERA

1.

What did my father see
through the deep black
tunnel as it sprung
slightly forward, clicked
its dark eye
closed, and got me
right there, rocking
on my rocking
horse, my first love,
legs tight, head back, sunlight
spotting my skin, pearls
through my hair.

2.

He must have sat
so still in my bedroom—
in the corner maybe, crouching,

trying to tame it,
that shiny monster
slung around his neck—
a reckless child, a baby.

3.

I call them art:
black and whites
of my three-year-old
love life. Legs rough
around my horse, fingers
pinching grass, face
buried in the laundry.

4.

Later it reminds her
of kissing. Her body
stuck in the hot room.
His voice: *stay still a minute*
then the tongue
she can't use to answer:
twisted wire
in the back of her throat.

DECEMBER

There were always days.
Numbered like the snowy hills
outside our window.
Snow frozen in caps
you could almost remove
like the hat from a baby's head.
    And the baby
inside my mother
would spin in her white globe:
a steady, patient rhythm
like rubbing wood for fire,
waiting for her father.

BOSTON NIGHT II

Pretend it was the first time he held her.
I mean gazed right into her eyes.
What if he found California in them:
butterflies, seashells, the sun—
obvious things you never let him love.
I know it wasn't raining,
but hear it, a tiny pattering on the window,
her newborn fingers greeting him.
Feel the rain open
that place in his throat you always wondered at
—though I know you only think of it now—
the red hollow of him. See it open
and your father start to cry.
You want to tell me you've never seen him cry.
It's too hard to picture.
Do it anyway. Do it for her
alone for the first time with him.
You can be there
the moment she knows
this is my father
though I can't tell you how she knew.
It was probably simpler than you think:

a soreness in her gums, her knees, the small of her
small back—but she knew.
She lifted her arm. She understood
she must reach for him.

II.

FRESH CUT

I owned the baby, the way I owned the lawn.

Mornings I'd take her there,
wrapped in her many blankets,
unwrap her, rock her
in its emerald fissures.

She was a wounded thing,
like fresh cut grass—
  wildflowers
when I crushed them
with my dense summer body.

What do you make of this love?

I wanted to bury her
in the cool dirt
under the weeping willow.

His branches, his mercy.

Afternoons, when the lawn
   began to burn
I'd roll to her; we'd lie
in deepest shade
among moss and mushrooms
alone with him.

JAR OF SEASHELLS

On a dusty bookshelf next to his keys,
his rubber-bands, a corkscrew.
Some were whole, some were crushed,
all were white, some had pink or gray spots,
all were his, he picked them
walking barefoot on the beach
after his body rose out of the foam.
He was alone, complete,
kelp in his hair, covered in salt.
He chose them, carried them in his hands,
carried them home, found the jar,
washed it, dried it, put them inside.
You didn't notice them at first,
they caught you off guard, you saw them
in that glance from the bookshelf
to the bedroom, the bookshelf
down the staircase, the bookshelf
out the sliding glass door—a flash,
an afterglow—when you looked for him
and he wasn't there.

REDWOOD CITY

If I could go there now, back to Redwood City,
back to my father's apartment, the first one
where he lived without us, would I
light them, one by one, all the dead
burners on his stovetop, or would I
stand there, as I do now, the kitchen door
tightly shut, all four burners leaking their poison
and suck it into my lungs:
the lovely smell of gas. It worries me.
I could let the kitchen fill with it.
A red protective film. My father.
My husband would be slouching on the sofa,
reading or sleeping, unaware
of what I do for love, what I do for him.
Anyway, his sense of smell is terrible,
which makes me wonder did my father
even smell it, or was he lost
in the sickening, gorgeous
carelessness that comes with being
entirely, dangerously alone.

THE INSIDE OF HOUSES

1.

Sometimes it was just me
alone in the house, surrounded by things:
newspaper on the floor to cover a spill,
check on the edge of the kitchen table,
my mother's book face down on the couch.
As long as I wanted, I would stare
and begin to sense—not the absence
or presence of a person—but what
remained: carelessness, their bravery
to have left something somewhere.

2.

Riding the train at night, if I was lucky
a woman would come to me:
white tablecloth, bottle of wine, high-chair, her fingers
resting on the windowsill, tapping.

3.

Because, really, it was the inside of houses
I wanted, empty of anyone who loved me:
yellow brush on the half-made bed
full of their hair, strand
after strand stuck to the sink—
where, in a fogged-up mirror
on a dark summer night, I began to notice
beauty—not in my face, not in my body,
but in the beating, humming
joy the earth felt when no one was there.

NIGHTGOWN

I remember the first time.
Her nightgown on the bathroom door,
lace blue, headstrong,
arms still folded at the elbows
to prove she'd been there:
a body, at night, with my father.
I remember first seeing
the woman that lived inside:
heavy against the door frame,
against my father, arms
rough, muscled—
like her lips the first time
I was told in my ear
to kiss them.

CALIFORNIA MAN

I'd sit with the other kids staring
at the dead grass, the railing,
waiting for him. He'd pull up
in his burgundy Cadillac, thick
with spicy smoke, the hum
of radio. He was driving us home.
The freeway was wide, cracked
in places, high stucco walls
on all sides. Some had murals:
women, jugs on their heads, kids
on their backs, Spanish warriors,
swords at their hips, blood
on their mouths. I was the one
who stared, the others
lost in homework; they'd all
lived here for years. I'd watch
his pipe, clenched, strange,
bobbing in the mirror, I'd think
this is California, where my father
took us, I live here, I'd say it
over and over. Then he stopped

in front of my apartment. He knew
just the spot.

        There she was,
my mother, leaning over the terrace,
gazing at the pavement.
She'd been waiting all day for me.
I'd get out, wouldn't say goodbye
to anyone, there wasn't time,
I had to run. Then I'd stand
on the hard, man-made
land that was suddenly ours.
Looking up, I'd ask her
to come down.

MARIPOSA AVENUE

Summer nights, my mother brought us carrots, peeled
in the great dark of the kitchen.

Hot and hungry, Dahlia and I
would sit on the stucco stairs
of the apartment that looked like a motel,
toes entwined, waiting for her.

Then she would come, holding
the carrots in her fingers, and gently,
because we knew how to hurt her, we would ask,
can we have a house, can we ever have
a garden? I wanted

butterflies to land on my fingers and Dahlia
to touch their pulsing wings,
brittle leaves to break against my palms, to
smooth the coarse remains down her cheeks.

There was a dirt I had never known.

She squeezed the carrots, and we could see
how chapped and tender
her fingers were, as if she'd spent days
digging in the earth.

Then quickly, because she knew
how hungry we were, she slid the carrots
between her fingers, and as they slipped
coolly into our mouths, we could love her.

OAKLAND, '89: AFTER THE EARTHQUAKE

Then they said there was a man.
He drove a Cadillac: blue, battered, stolen.
He waits for you. He's got candy.
They taped his picture to the blackboard:
dirty blond, blue eyes, pock-faced.
He could have been thirteen.

Joni would grab me after school,
corner me next to the rotting rhododendron,
lift her sleeve, flex her tiny bicep.
I'll protect you.
She was skin and muscle,
no softness anywhere, a child.

I walked staring at the cracks
in the pavement, the different shapes
of tragedy. One so deep and jagged
you could see through
to the soil, its black, gnarled roots.
In another—smaller, less deliberate—
grass had started growing.

I thought I saw him once.
Looking up, a blur of blue and yellow,
then a car, then a man, but
his skin was clear as water—he was
holding a baby. His baby. I could see it
in their smiles.

Joni thought it was funny, this game of looking.
Then she would forget and the world
would turn to Mike.
Michael. He smiles like an angel.

His eyes were angel blue,
so clear, if he let me
I could see into his brain—
whatever it looked like
I wanted to see. Then,
if he wanted, he could see
me, under my clothes,
whatever it looked like.

There were new words:
fault line, magnitude, after shock.
Epicenter was my favorite.
Nights I'd say it thinking of him.

The two plates banging together.
They said it even happened
in the ocean.

I wanted the ocean. Light, rushing
through me. I'd start to drift
across the bridge. Sinking
into sand, I'd feel it.

He was there. I'd take him,
clasp him to the center
of my chest, his ear pressed to me like
I was the shell you hear the ocean with.

I had that power.

PENNIES

One afternoon, after he'd left, when he was more
man than father, in his one-room apartment, garbage
rising from the basement, though I had stopped
being a child, anyone's child, I crawled
under the bed, chin on the cold wood floor, and found them
in their cracked bowl; I peeled off the layers
of spider webs, blew off the dust, and there it was,
my father's wealth, dimly flickering.

FIRST BLOOD

It was mild, the night I stood
over my sister's sleeping body

and felt, for the first time, she was
mine. It was like the ocean

had come, swept away
the floor, the ceiling, the beds—

only she was saved,
the sheets foaming, slipping

off her. Then, when it built
and built in me, dropped a little—

not quite red yet, the way water
takes on no single color—

I remembered the egg
two weeks before, rising:

opal, slick, silver,
a glass eye that saw her

believing in me, craving me,
the way children need light.

EAST

In the end, I left him:
my California, my father, my love.
Or rather, we left him:
my mother, my sister, me.
So three women left one man,
each a wisp of fog
between the Redwoods.

III.

BRIDE

You couldn't have seen—
I was a child—how my father
looked at me, tender
in my yellow dress, filmed me
wading in that creek, its gray
slick stones. Barefoot,
I walked across them
though they weren't fire
though the creek I wobbled over
holding onto nothing
was not a threshold—I ran
to my father's arms.
He barely touched me.
I was like the negatives
he knelt over in the darkroom
in the basement where his fingers
glazed the edges,
the flimsy parameters.
No one saw—I waited
hours shivering, the hollow
basement stairs, yellow
wrinkled dress slipping

off, black night
tunneling, waiting.
I began to wait for you.

FOURTEEN IN HIS ATTIC

I can picture him then, my husband
examining me, hands deep inside,
digging, my body a puzzle
of the unexplored world. He did it
over and over, until he
cracked me, my code, my too hot
to touch, my body brimming, my—
he wouldn't stop. Then
it poured, twisted
out of me: coral, tree stumps,
powdered silk of broken
stars—there might have been
more—and I
just lay there, dumb,
as though all he'd discovered,
uncovered, touched and touched
meant nothing, was a memory
I didn't remember—he
couldn't stop, what did I expect
of him, hardly a man, hungry—

ENDYMION

You, boy in the faded green t-shirt
slouching in the lawn chair
outside the laundromat—
Wake up. It's me.
Remember? It was summer,
night, like now, but you
took me, my hand, led me
from your beat-up Honda,
clutched, dragged me
through gravel, sand, moved me
to hot dusk. I remember you
turned me in the dark toward
something like water,
streaks of silver, pulled, streamed me,
I was water. I often ask
how could I be water
but it was like that then.
You remember. You dissolved
into me. I drowned. Here,
in these plastic yellow bags
I offer you oranges. How else

can I repay you?   They are cold.

They will cool you.

I have nothing else to offer.

MARRIAGE VOW

I begin by telling you I have nothing
but earth. Look at my eyes:
the muddy center. See it
rumble. And the car
skidding on steamy asphalt—
it's the black, dirt caked
road that thrills me.
Would you watch—my skin,
my bones—if I
rolled on it? You could
taste me. Salty. Absolute.
This is what I know. Stare
at my sandal straps,
all that hold me
down. Fireflies, dust—
they spin in fevered
air. They rise. They're
what will remain of me.
You have come this far.
It's amazing you can
stand still and look at me.
Soon you'll take this

hollow hand. Lead me
away. The earth, its human
heart. You will need it.

EQUINOX

I want to tell you
about the wounded world.

In California, my mother missed the seasons.

That's why it hurts
when the leaves begin to change,
each red leaf a sliver
of her heart.

But I also find it
beautiful. Because I love
to watch her pain
blooming on the street.

The way, these hazy mornings,
it rises in my throat.

Sometimes I think it will fly,
a white dove, my father,
out of my mouth.

Can you understand my silence
as I wander through the kitchen?

Mostly she missed the dark.
Craved the stars. I miss

lying with you, in deepest
summer, before the trees
began to bleed.

FALL

The kitchen sink, each fat drop slowly pulsing—
cars glide by, leaves loosen from branches,
everything sounds too much like music and soon
your heavy body will move up the stairs
to me and I will ask you
why you're here, who you love.

THINKING OF MY FATHER

I lean between our plants,
cheek against the cold window.
I breathe with them, their wet skin:
how a baby breathes
with her mother. Then I catch
a glimpse of the garden:
someone else's, gleaming, tender,
a large dark square of green.

Falling asleep with you,
I remember something swinging—
a chime, a branch?—and how I wanted
to rock and rock forever.

LULLABY

The fights are like trains
flying past houses
   and how I love
riding, window seat, gazing:
sneakers, hangers, tulips,
a baby carriage half buried
in a heap of tires—
quick stops over bridges
   when you lie
suspended over everything
and you're never sure
if they forgot her,
the baby, just left her there
sleeping—or was it simply
sunflowers you saw
peeking through tires.

A HUSBAND'S THINGS

1. Pens, Newspaper, Paper Clips
I think he likes to look at each thing separately,
there on the rug. He despises mixing—
for instance, if everything were to go
in that backpack, on his desk.
No. Each thing must be accounted for.
The way, since childhood,
he makes a line on his plate
dividing one food from another.
Nights, I watch. How careful he is
that nothing will touch.

2. Cell Phone Charger
Each morning, after he's left, the long cord
snaking from the outlet, up the wall
to the bookshelf, its small square head
waiting for him.

3. Long Sleeved Shirts
Through fogged glass I see them
ink-blue, blood-red,
daring in the dryer—
twisting, tangling, knotting
my sweater, jeans, dresses,
as though he has that many arms.

4. Video Tapes
When he thinks I'm sleeping,
he slides one in, presses the button.
All night a small red light
floods the room, the back of my eye.
I dream of fish, that I'm a fish
and I've lost my husband.

5. Peter Pan Coloring Book
Some things are for children.
But he buys them anyway, like the plastic lizard
I found in my jacket pocket.
He buys them, I think, to tease me
back to childhood. He wants me
to see him, there on the couch, Peter.
Peter, he wants me to say.

ON YOUR PARENTS' STOOP

Next came the part I couldn't explain.
So I said to you, in the white
January morning: It was never
my father; I was afraid, I don't know,
to be alive. And you said:
I think I know. Then
it was August, your mother's azaleas
brown, heavy to the ground
because she was leaving,
and we were married, and you said:
Let's go home now. And we did
because it was ours.

IV.

FOUR DREAMS

1. I Saw Your Heart
All I did was lift your Batman shirt.
It wasn't beating. It was frozen
in time so I could study it.
But all I remembered was the gold
or the fire, how I could look at it.
Your heart. It smelled like you.

2. I Had Milk
You came home in your baseball hat
like nothing had changed, slid it off,
stood above me, dropped it
crumpled in my lap. Then
you lay on the long blue couch—
head against my sleeve dreaming
of milk and your heart
flicked as if we had a child
but I only had milk.

3. You Were My Child
Then for hours we lay
on the couch playing Scrabble.
I was teaching you words:
letters mixing in your mouth.
You yanked my sweater zipper.
You were bored.
Afternoon filled our throats.
We were alone.

4. I Spied on You
In the dark night holding
a baby, still in its gold
sac, kind of floating there
on your chest. I saw you
face each other: father and son
through the tissues, drifting,
breathing, just breathing, and looking.

WE WENT TO THE MOON

My sister and I. But it was only the moon
filling the Parkwood Pool and we weren't
sisters. We bolted up the ramps,
climbed the steep white steps—
mothers' voices claimed us
but we didn't look back. We peeked
under the gate, between the bars.
How strangely it swayed there:
bloated, forgiving
over tense blue ripples.

Then I knew
her cold hand was cold
for a reason and it didn't matter
who she was. I had touched her.
I couldn't let go.

FIELD

Mornings I shut my eyes
and it all comes back:
wild poppies, sunset, far from home.
Baby on my stomach, not
my sister, but like her—
the way, certain hours, she resembles
me. Both of us
just lying there, maybe
we're sleeping, rocking
as the earth rocks, reddening
in our cores.
         And I feel
between my shoulders, how it felt
in childhood, to suddenly want
something strange and living,
but I don't know what.

Wendy Wisner teaches writing at Hunter College, where she received her MFA in poetry. She was the recipient of an Academy of American Poets Prize and the 2003 Amy Award. Her poems have appeared in *Runes, Sojourner, 5 AM,* and other journals. She lives in Brooklyn with her husband.